The **Spiritual Wisdom** of **Kids**

Deborah Masters & Robert Rabbin

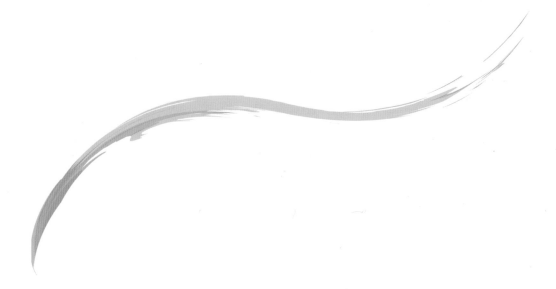

Global Truth Publishing
Mill Valley, California

Global Truth Publishing
20 Sunnyside Avenue, Suite A-116
Mill Valley, CA 94941-1928 USA
415.263.4829
sales@globaltruthpublishing.com

ISBN 0-9740465-0-7
Library of Congress Control Number:
2003092352
First Printing 2003

Cover, book design, and illustrations
by Claudia Uscátegui

Wholesale discounts are available to
resellers and special discounts are
available on bulk purchases of this book
for educational and fundraising purposes
and for use as premiums, incentives, and
promotions. For details, please contact
the publisher.

Table of Contents

Acknowledgments

This book is dedicated to all children everywhere—may you inherit a
world worthy of your wisdom.

We offer our heartfelt gratitude and deepest thanks to:

The 123 kids who graciously consented to be interviewed for this book.
May you all enjoy unlimited blessings throughout your lives. It should
be noted here that they preferred to be called "kids" rather
than "children."

The parents, guardians, grandparents, uncles and aunts, cousins, and
friends of these kids who supported this project with love.

The many generous people and organizations who helped us bring this
book to life: Eric Traub, Abra Greenspan, Leslie Herrick, Doug Ivey,
The Freedom Project, Richard Moscarello, Rabbi Sydney Mintz,
Teri Hollowell, Randy Davis, Nick Jans, Sandra Rabbin,
Susan Greenwood, Devika Brandt, Deborah Erwin, Buddy Zais,
Joan Bekins, Karen Weissman, Claire Papin, Rebekah Laros,
Sharon Barnett, Debbie Grillo, Miles Riley, Matthew Mitchell, and
Sophia Scorcia for her love and inspiration.

Siena Hood, Zoe Loughran Brezsny, Elsinore Smidth, and
Lauren Moscarello, for their marvelous poems.

Deborah's family, for their love: Violet and George Porterfield, Charlotte
Dempsey, Gladys Mock, Alvin and Ruth Retzer, and Judy Lombardi.

Amy Kahn, for her love and for her compassionate copyediting of the
entire manuscript. Her editorial eyes are otherworldly.

Jonathan Burstein (www.jburstein.com), for his exquisite portraits,
showcased in the Epilogue.

Claudia Uscátegui (www.cudesignstudios.com), our dear friend and
resident genius, for her cover and book design and illustrations.
Claudia was an integral part of the creative alchemy that produced this
book; she drank daily from a magical potion of inspiration and
dedication. Her contributions to this project were numerous and
enormous, as are her sense of humor and beautiful spirit.

There is a story of a 3-year-old who leans into the crib of her infant sister, whispering, "Tell me again what God looks like. I'm starting to forget." If a 3-year-old is already starting to forget, what might we grown-ups have forgotten about what God looks like through a child's eyes, and from a child's state of innocence and vulnerability? The 123 kids that we interviewed for this book are still glowing with the light from whence we all come, and so they speak with a clear remembrance of important and sacred things. Their wisdom can be our teacher. Their purity deserves to be honored. Their innocence should become our conscience.

The wisdom of these kids is characterized by simplicity, depth, feeling, and originality. They speak from a place of natural and sacred connection to others, to animals, to Mother Earth—to life. They speak with an authority and a directness that are compelling. We have much to learn from them.

Enjoy their every word, but read slowly and carefully. Their words deserve consideration and contemplation; they are legitimate spiritual lessons that echo the great teachers of all traditions throughout history. You will find the classic themes of spiritual life freshly painted and newly presented—themes of love and death, sanctity and reverence, peace and nonviolence, connection and oneness. They speak often of love: the word and the feeling arise in them easily and naturally. They thrive in loving and being loved, and see love as the organizing principle of life. And so they speak to those of us who have lost our feeling for love and forgotten the power of love. They speak of what God looks and feels like in many different ways; and they see God *in* all things and *as* all things. And so they speak to those of us whose narrow definition of God separates and polarizes one people from another, and all people from nature.

Without exception, the kids are appalled at the very idea of war and violence. They ask again and again to be able to live in the quiet comforts and safety of true and enduring peace. And so they speak to those of us who are too quick and even eager to wage war, and to those who profit from war. The kids speak of keeping the Earth clean

Introduction

Introduction

and pure. And so they speak to those of us who think the Earth is our personal dumping ground. They speak of the beauty and power and sacredness of animals, and of how we must preserve their habitats. They speak of the need to preserve forests. And so they speak to those of us who ransack nature for profit without regard for the consequences of our plundering. They speak of enjoying the gift of life, of having fun. And so they speak to those among us who have forgotten how to play or feel the passion of pure living. They speak of looking for the goodness in people's hearts, of treating people well, and of being kind and generous. And so they speak to all of us. We have much to learn from them.

Who are these kids? They are from 2 to 13 years of age, from diverse ethnic origins and backgrounds and economic strata. We interviewed most of the kids in person, others on the phone, and a few interviews were sent in by parents who spoke with their children on our behalf. In all cases, they did not know in advance what we were going to ask them; their responses were spontaneous, and yet deeply considered. With rare exception, we did not editorially "improve" the kids' language. We wanted to let you read their words in their natural, uncensored voices. We used an extremely informal style of capitalization, punctuation, and other grammatical conventions, in order to reflect the kids' own informal speaking styles and rhythms, which were often flowing and cascading like streams and waterfalls of excitement and imagination and breathless exuberance. We could not use everything that each child said because of our chapter themes and space considerations. But whether a child contributed one line or many, each contribution, like each child, is unique and precious.

During the course of our interviews, four distinct themes emerged: *God, Love, Peace,* and *Healing.* The book has thus been divided into those four sections. It seems to us that the visions and ideals of the first three sections find realization and actualization in the fourth section. In this last section, *Healing,* the kids put their values to work; they offer specific prescriptions for bringing the world into harmony with the universal principles expressed by them in *God, Love,* and *Peace.*

The poet Rumi once said, "Take on a big project, like Noah." Such a project is suggested by the kids: make the world a safe and beautiful place for all children, and for their children. Truly, this would be a project worthy of Noah, would it not? This world should be a playground of safety, opportunity, and peace for *every child alive:* all sizes, all colors, all nationalities, all races, all religions, all everything. It should be a great place for them. Sadly, many places in this world are not such playgrounds, but rather barren fields of poverty and starvation, battlegrounds strewn with landmines, and dark alleys where children are exploited in terrible ways. This should not be. It is not right. We have a lot of work to do to restore the natural order of things. It will be a big project, but we can't think of a more important one: to make this world safe for every child alive. We will have an easier time of it if we let the spiritual wisdom of kids show us how.

And, finally, to the kids: We love you. We respect you. We honor you. We thank you. Please know that we will work long and hard to make this world a safe and beautiful place for you.

Robert Rabbin & Deborah Masters
May 2003

As we grow older, we often lose our appreciation for qualities such as *awe, wonder, mystery,* and *magic,* perhaps thinking they must be put aside as "things of a child." This is tragic, for if we do this, we will become dogmatic in our views, our heart will lose its luster, and our spirit, its shine. When our inner light lessens, we get angry. And then we start arguing, and then fighting— about all kinds of things, especially about God. And fighting about God is not good.

These kids know this and they will have none of it. Their intimacy with God is profound, and their bold stories of God's nature and powers enchanted us. We were thrilled to learn that God "looks like Abraham Lincoln" and "has long curly hair down her back, a toe ring and a brown cat with a beard" and "doesn't shoot green slime out of his ears." We learned that God is love and peace, cloud and wind, mouse and mountain, heaven and Mother Earth, male and female. We were told that God is "bigger than anything."

Isn't this wonderful news? There is room for everyone and space for all. There is no need to get angry, argue, or fight.

*The "correct" answer:
God is...U!

QUIZ*
God is...?
(Please circle the correct answer.)

A   **good and handsome**
B   the universe
C   **someone in my heart**
D   a sparkly flower
E   **love**
F   a friend to us all
G   **a chipmunk and a skier**
H   Mother Earth
I   **within all of us**
J   the whole world
K   **hope**
L   the creator
M   **the biggest angel**
N   all around us
O   **the wind**
P   a mouse
Q   **a homeless man**
R   a special kind of cloud
S   **standing behind you, Mama**
T   no one knows
U   **all of the above**

I think of God as an **angel** or a **sparkly beautiful flower.**
Emmy Wagner, 12

G

is a word of **hope.**
Angelique Traub, 12

God is **bigger** than anything.

Sophia Scorcia,

God is every thing

God is not necessarily a **"he"** or **"she"**; it's the **universe**, the **atmosphere**. If God were a picture, God would be a **scene of nature** showing the broad heavens and stars.

Zoe Loughran Brezsny, 12

God is not a boy or a girl, it's kind of a spirit that some people believe in, that sometimes people can like talk to it, in their minds. It's up in the sky. A lot of people love it and look up to it. I go to Sunday school and Hebrew school and we talk to God a lot. God helps in some way. We pray to him.

Cortnay Cymrot, 10

God is right here and right here, to the left and right of me, and under and above me. It's a boy, even though I know it's not; it's always referred to as a "he," so it reinforces in my mind that it's a boy. But I know it's not. But they refer to him with a capital "h." I don't think God is a person or a human. He is everything. God is in the clouds and he is looking down and he is on the ground looking up and he is in this room and he can be wherever you imagine him to be.

Chelsea Cymrot, 12

God is a mythical human who created us all and the Earth. God watches over us and makes everything happen I'd say God hangs out in heaven…and in our hearts.

Spencer Palmer, 10

God is when you go on vacation. God lives up in the sky. Angels look invisible. They fly around in the sky with a wing.

Alexander Palmer, 5

God is the controller of the world and the peacemaker. God is in heaven and he looks like a very smart and brave person.

Lauren Christianson, 10

God looks kind of like Abraham Lincoln. He has a beard. You shouldn't tell funny stuff about God.

Marcus Christianson, 6

God is in everything and God made everything
and everything is special the way that it
is because it's different. God is in plants and
people and rocks.

Danny Sacks, 11

God is a very helpful spirit. God is everything;
there's a little of God in everything. Nobody
knows if God's a person or a thing, but it's
so said that God is a spirit. God is many spirits
for many religions and God primarily helps us.
God helps to bring peace; he tries to bring
peace everywhere. I pray for food and to thank
him that we're living and to thank him that he
made us and for making the world that we can
live in. He made our world for us to live in.

Alon Sacks, 9

I've heard many different stories about God, but
I think he is the Creator and he created
everything on the Earth and he created us.
God's really important and I believe that he
created everything and we should be
respectful of him and pray to him and thank
him.

Elliott Stone, 12

God is a cloud and he walks on them. God
helps people; he makes them walk and makes
them move. I talk to God in my bed. God
makes me feel good.

Aaron Stone, 8

God is the Creator that created everything: trees, people, knowledge. God gives you hands, arms, a body, and a mind so you can live. God lives on the other side, in the spirit world.

Thomas Medicinehorse, 12

God is a spirit that keeps you living. God is many things; he could be your hair. God is in the Arctic Ocean. God is everything.

Eleanor Silverstein, 9

God is air. God is air

Lucia Simon, 6

God is a powerful ruler that can do great things. God helps the blind so they can see, and helps people to walk, and brings the dead back to life. God lives in heaven and with us.

Kylee Larsen, 12

I like the idea there is God and that everything that happens is supposed to happen and that you can't stop something from happening. Destiny is cool because something already is going to happen to you and you know it's going to happen to you; but the other part is that it feels weird that you can't control your life because of destiny. I believe that you can change your destiny. You are still going to go in one direction instead of another one, but you can bend it a little bit.

Ciro Podany, 12

Sometimes when someone in my family dies, I think about where they go. So sometimes I think about God and how he watches over everybody. I think God lives in the heavens, somewhere in outer space. Sometimes I dream of going to heaven and there's this big arch and that's God's house. I don't really know what happens in heaven since I haven't been there; but I imagine that it's a place with flowers and you can do anything you want, like fly.

Alexandra Goldstein, 10

I think that God is a power,
an energy source of some kind.
I really feel good about God,
and I know that God is cool.
God brings peace and
love to Earth.

Connor Barnett, 8

God is love and spirit.

Amanda Slaughter, 10

Spirit is light. Everyone has **light** in them.

God takes care of people and keeps them
company in heaven. People in heaven watch
over us. Angels are like my grandma and
grandpa; they stand on clouds and watch over
their grandchildren because they love them.
It makes me happy to know that my grandma and
grandpa are watching over me.

Lucia Barnett, 7

God belongs to the chapel and
he loves little children. Jesus is a baby.
Children love Jesus. God is a king.
Angels belong to Christmas and
they are happy.

Audrey Norton, 4

God talks to me in my dreams. He said good stuff.
Sometimes he tells me what I'm going to do
the next day. God is a friend to us all and nice,
and I hope he never leaves us.
God is good and handsome.

Joshua Slaughter, 8

God is more of a thought, so I think people just turn that thought into an actual person, because it's easier for people to believe in; rather than people just believing in a feeling, they can more look towards a person. I don't talk to God but I sometimes feel…not alone, like walking down a hallway.

Angelique Traub, 12

I think God is me because whenever I go to sleep I feel him down in my heart. It feels kind and loving.

Lilly Barnett, 7

I bring God into my heart through prayer. I start with "Dear Lord, please come into my heart and forgive me for my sins, in Jesus' name. Amen." When you accept God into your heart you feel his love and grace. Sometimes you'll feel him pushing at your heart. Do what he tells you; say he's trying to lead you somewhere, go there. Sometimes you'll have an experience and God uses that experience to shape you. People should appreciate how good life is, and appreciate God because we wouldn't be here without him.

Timothy Josh Royal, 10

I think the most important thing in life is to love God with all your heart—even if you don't, he loves you. Personally, I think because of that, you should love him. The reason you can love is because of God. You can love other people because of God. A person who loves God cares more about every little thing, every little living creature, and they know that God created that creature. They also know that every single one of the humans on the face of this Earth is created in God's image, and that makes me not prejudiced—knowing that I'm created to look just like God, just like you are, and everybody is. It says in the Bible that if you love God with all your heart and all your soul, he'll give you more love to give others.

Amy Elizabeth Royal, 12

I think that God is more of a **spiritual force** that lives in everything; **it is everything.** I don't think God's a "he." I don't think it's any one thing. I think it can be **whatever anyone wants it to be, many shapes and forms.**

My dad's not that religious, but once his plane got hit by lightning, and he thought there was a bomb or something— he said a little prayer to God. Eric Brandon, 13

God means a *spirit* or the creator of Earth.

Elena Scott, 12

God is **peaceful, loving.** He's good. God is in our hearts. I talk to God to tell him I'm sorry about something.

Afton Wight, 8

God is the **whole world, even you.**
God helps the world to survive and grow.

Zoe Goldberg, 6

God is **powerful**. God makes things grow and gives us food.

God is something that keeps me **safe** and **happy.**

Lila Hood, 8

God is someone who **helps you.**
He brings lots of things to Earth
ke plants and trees and animals and people.

Elena Bakar, 8

Matthew Schabel, 7

God is looking over us, and his spirit is up in heaven.

Liesel Staubitz, 6

God is full of love and wants
to help us in every way possible,
but he lets us go through
different experiences so
we can love, get angry, and
show our emotions.
God's everywhere, in everyone.
God takes half of himself and
puts it in everyone so that they
have a **spirit** and can live and walk.
God's in every living thing:
plants, animals, people.

Justin Jones, 11

God is a person who was a king. Jesus' dad was God. Jesus is God's son. Jesus was nice to everybody. He never killed anybody and he never hurt anybody. He takes care of people up in heaven like Auntie Naomi and our dog Tessie. Auntie Naomi got very sick. Her name is my middle name. Grandma Mutzenberger is up there too. I love them and I miss them a lot. They are very happy in heaven because everyone is nice in heaven. God is someone in my heart. He takes care of people in heaven and makes sure people don't fight. People don't ever fight in heaven because it is magical. When you die you go up to heaven and you get wings. The ones you showed me on your back will get bigger when you get there. There are a lot of angels in heaven. In a book that Daddy and I read, when an animal goes to heaven then the kid angels take care of them. One had a pretty white bird and one had a white rabbit. Do you think one of them has Tessie?

God was a healer when he was alive. He healed people. He touched them and they were good and one time they were cheeters—no not cheeters—I can't remember—it's like a cheetah—they were very sick and they had sores all over them. *[Madison was trying to remember the word "lepers" and was relating it to the animal "leopard," but in her mind she got it confused with the word "cheetah" and came up with the word "cheeters."]* The guy told them to get really dirty and they had to stand on the road and they had to stop the people from going. They said "not clean" and no one wanted them because they had sores and there was one person who was a leper so he asked God to make him good again and a long time ago he said I can't heal you and a little bit later he said you can heal anything and he touched him and he was like other people. He was a healer and he can heal anyone. When you are very sick he can sometimes heal you. I think he puts power down here *[in your heart]* and makes you feel good.

Madison Naomi Schobinger, 6

I think God and Jesus came here to better understand what we do and help us learn to do a lot of hard things and help us through hard times— because when we pray they help us.

TJ Dempsey, 11

God lives very very high in heaven and everywhere, like in the sky floating around. God is one big spirit that watches over everyone and tries to make sure that everyone is okay. I talk to God at Christmas and all different kinds of holidays and when war is going on right now. I would pray to him because my cousins are in the army and I hope that everyone who is in the army and all the military forces are okay right now.

Kaylie Kathleen Williams, 10

God gives hope to people and gives them a reason to help others. God lives in people's minds. I believe God gives hope to a lot of people and that's good.

Stewart Gruen, 11

God is the Creator. He is everywhere; he is in every living thing. He is good luck, good fortune. Before a test, I say "I hope I get a good grade." People should try and be nicer, because if you're praying to God and you're being a bad person, he wouldn't listen to your calls. Rabbis and priests are usually more kind than the average people on the street, because they are more at one with God. It's what they do for a living, to be wise and smart and to make people feel better.

Adrian Franco, 11

God is something that created the Earth and helps things be right, and I think he's in every space and I'd say he's in your heart, because you love him—and that whatever he is, he is really really great.

Ari Bental, 9

God will protect you from harmful things, keep you healthy, protect your loved ones. All things happen for a reason, and most things will always happen because God chose them to happen; they don't happen by accident.
Ariel Filane, 12

God speaks to you an

I would say that everything has its own little spirit, a spirit that would help a plant grow or help somebody open their eyes. But I don't think there's some big God that rules everybody and tells them what to do. I think that there are little fairies. Everyone has inside of them their own spirit that makes them grow.

Elsinore Smidth, 13

Now that I'm young, I think of God as a thing. Not everyone believes in God. God will do things and he doesn't need your thanks, but it's polite to thank him. But God will just do things for you even without your thanks.
Sophie Gilchrist, 11

O God! O Lord! O Creator of all living beings—I thank thee for all thou hast bestowed upon us and all thou will bestow upon us in the future. God is mighty and powerful.
Lauren Grieve, 8

I believe in God and I believe in Christ. God and Christ mean love. Love is caring and respect and helping.

Michelle Leason, 10

I think everyone has a little bit of God in them. He's in all different kinds of things.

Albert Brown, 8

ys in a tree that is fire, "You better appear."

Gabriel Newbrun-Mintz, 2

The Dalai Lama is a God.

Theo Chamberlain, 3

God is a person that loves you a lot.

Gayle Henry, 12

God's not a person because the wind is God. The wind loves me 'cause that's his Creator above him, 'cause the Creator lets every person see him. About God, he likes you back because he's so nice, 'cause he lets you do every single thing to him. God loves you very much 'cause he lets you love him. Clouds could turn into different things and something comes from the sky, 'cause the wind makes it wavy so we could do stuff like put our umbrellas underneath our heads.

Malia Kristina Bertelsen, 4

God is a special kind of cloud
in the sky that helps dead people.
God is a man and a woman.
The man makes boys and the woman
makes girls. They have a house made
of clouds and eat rain. There is a hole
in the house which lets the sun shine in
to light up the house.
God has long long gray hair and a
beard and the woman God has long
curly hair down her back.
God has a toe ring and a
brown cat with a beard.

Samantha Collins, 7

I mostly think of God as sort of in the wind, but also in the clouds, and in heaven. God is a majestic grown man but not exactly—he's also transparent.

Terry Castleman, 9

I think God is someone who watches over you all the time. He could be like a person, but also like everything else. If you saw a mouse, it could be God looking at you. God is really in everything.

Jacob Dorfman, 8

God created things for us and we're really thankful for him. I talk to God once in a while at our table. God helps the world, he makes food for us, he made trees to help us live, and he made an atmosphere.

Quincy Engelbrecht, 7

I think of God as an angel or a sparkly beautiful flower. He created me and my family and there would be no world without God. So, be happy and love life. Don't fight in war, but instead be thankful for family, love, and God.

Emmy Wagner, 12

Sometimes I make wishes to God for a nice friend. God is a friendly spirit. It feels that God is alive, and I know that God is made of love.

Mallory Bragg, 8

I think God is really old and he has a lot of wrinkles and he's part of church. **I think about God.** I actually think that God did make the world. I know that God made people.

Katherine Mary Scotnicki, 5

God looks like a skier and a chipmunk.

Nicole Childers, 5

Coco, I love you. I hope you have a fun time with God up in heaven. I miss you. I will see you when I die too, but it will take a long time for me to die. Coco is one of God's creatures and God looks after all his creatures.

Gigi Staubitz, 4

God is
the biggest angel
in the world.
He looks like
he is our father
and he is.
He is all around us.
He is standing
behind you,
Mama.
He is watching
over us.

Victoria Berggren, 7

God is bigger
than anything.
He doesn't shoot
green slime
out of his ears.

Sophia Scorcia, 4

If I feel bad
and I want to talk
to someone,
I talk to God.
Sometimes
God answers.

*Roza Trilesskaya, 8
(Nastasia Bayer
translated from Russian)*

God is a perfect person who can do anything he wants. God is in heaven and everywhere and in everybody.

Jeremiah Byers, 12

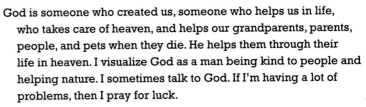

God is someone who created us, someone who helps us in life,
who takes care of heaven, and helps our grandparents, parents,
people, and pets when they die. He helps them through their
life in heaven. I visualize God as a man being kind to people and
helping nature. I sometimes talk to God. If I'm having a lot of
problems, then I pray for luck.

Evan Cranston, 9

God is like a creature in the sky and he's just all around everywhere
and he can look at everything that is going on and he creates
everything and everybody. He's so big that he's in every space
and he's watching everybody and he knows what's going on.
God helps you.

Robert Lehmann, 9

God is always with you. You could pray to him if you feel lonely.
God warns you if you stay close to him; if something weird
is going to happen, he warns you to stay away from wherever, or
don't go to that place you're going to. God is everywhere. We
should be more close to God. If you're not doing bad things, you
are closer to God.

Molly McCann, 10

Most people think about miracles, or things that you can't
explain with anything from science, so that's where God comes
along. God is miracles, another idea besides science. God is
what happens when nothing else can explain it.

Lilah Clevey, 11

What does God look like? That's kind of a tricky one. God is our father and he will always forgive us. God is always ready to listen and hear what you have to say. God is very peaceful and helping.
Leah Grillo, 8

No one knows what God really is, but he's mostly everywhere. If you do something bad, he's probably watching you.
Aaron Smith, 9

God is a person who watches over us and you look up to him when you need him. I pray that my grandma and my grandpa are all right, and for my uncle when he goes on trips.
Kylee Koenig, 12

God—*she's* a person who lives in heaven and you can always trust *her* and look up to *her* because *she'll* always be there. I talk to God when there's something bad happening in my family and ask *her* to heal them up.
Jill Meserve, 11

God is probably a boy, because our prayers talk about God like he is. But I think he's just invisible. He lives in the wind and in heaven. He lives everywhere. I think he has powers, but I don't believe that he really parted the Red Sea.

Marshall Levensohn, 9

God is really nice and takes care of us. I think
God is like this: when you go to heaven,
the boys go to the boy God, and the girls go to
the girl God, and whatever kind of animals, say
my dog, when he dies, he goes to the doggie
God. When my bunny dies, he goes to the
bunny God, and when my bird dies, he goes to
the bird God, and so on and so on. God
makes them into a new person and they come
back as a different person.

A girl God might look like all the girls in the world.
She might have different parts of our bodies, like
she might have freckles for me and some other
people that have freckles and then curly hair or
straight hair. Maybe she likes to wear different
color blush or makeup. Same with the boys.

God could be anything and protect everybody.
God could be my dog right now; he can
just shrink into my dog and when he wants to
go back up, he can just go back up.
Danielle Schatzman, 8

Angels are a kind of bird, an angel bird, and they fly. *Abbie Benford, 5*

God is everything alive. He

God is someone who creates things and people too.

God is Mother Earth so we should take care of her. *Lucy Black, 6*

God might be a cloud. Anya Rauchle, 6

Ben Herrick, 11

t one person, one animal, one tree. He is within all of us, within our soul.

akes everything grow and everything live. *Indigo George, 7*

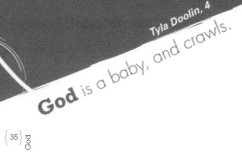

Tyla Doolin, 4

God is a baby, and crawls.

When I think of **God** I think of many Gods. There is a lot of them, not just one main God. They can have some say on what happens on Earth, but they don't have all the say; they just have a little extra powers.

Sarah Wiener, 13

God is a spirit. I don't think he's completely perfect because of the world he's made. If God did make the world, he's kind of weird because he made it all weird, because everyone's fighting and it's not peaceful.

Luke Garrison, 13

I do believe that whatever **God** is, it is good, so maybe God is love.

Lauren Moscarello, 8

The biggest problem in the world is religion because there are all these wars going on because people think that one person is a **God** and other people think that's a lie and so I think there's not really one God but it's really like the God in you.

Siena Hood, 12

God made everyone alive, so we should treat each other nice. **God** lives in the sky really far away. We can't see him. God lives inside us too.

Caleb Mahoney, 6

God is everything that is beautiful.
If you see a pretty flower, it's God.
If you see a homeless man
that has a twinkle in his eye, that's God.
Anything or anyone that is special to you
is in some way God.

Julia Egger, 13

Unknown, unseen, felt

you come from above

where stars always shine

light surrounds you inside and out

you give the fruit of your soul

to the people

and

embroider a sorrowful heart

a smile is life giving

your hands soothe a

worried face

like a ripple in a stream

you flow in and out of life

Siena Hood, 12

Amy Elizabeth Royal says, "The reason you can love is because of God." According to the kids, there is a direct relationship between God and love. They seem to say that love is the very presence of God; love is how we know God exists. As Gabriel Newbrun-Mintz—all of 2 years old—says, "Love means God makes you hug each other." This section confirms the highest teaching of all religions and spiritual traditions: God and love are one and the same.

During the interviews, we learned that love is not a concept or ideal; it is the living and visible bond of oneness that connects each of us to the other and to all things in existence. Juan Bernardo Uscátegui, 4 years old, says, "Love is strength, hope, the heart, the value of life…" The kids know these things as a matter of fact. They thrive in love and wither without it. They need love. They want love.

They are as quick to give love as be loved, knowing full well that each feeds the other. In their world, love is made real through action: there are hugs and kisses without end, caring and helping are automatic, trust and safety essential. Love, love, and LOVE.

Love is the value of life. Give love. Receive love. That is all. Class dismissed.

Love is a feeling that you should give away.

Albert Brown, 8

L O

The light inside everyone is called **love.**

Liesel Staubitz, 6

It's importan
all have families. W
We shoul

Love is

strength, **hope,**
the heart,
the value of life,
the ability,
the innocence.
Lucia and I give each other kisses of love.

Juan Bernardo Uscátegui, 4

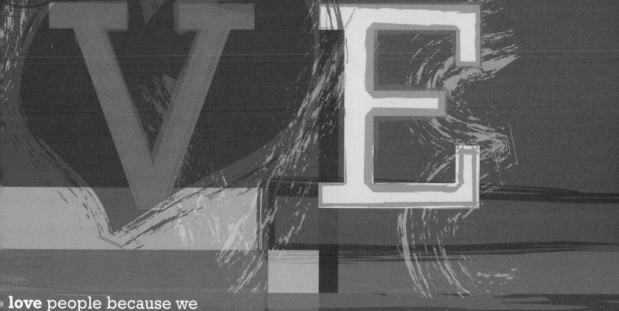

love people because we
should all **take care** of babies.
love each other, and...

's not okay if you don't brush your teeth.

Isabel Rauchle, 3

If I love someone...

...it means that I am not alone.
Moki Kawaguchi, 8

...I would care for them and be nice to them.
Emma Lynch, 8

...it means that they are in my heart and they keep me safe and that they love me back, I hope.
Elena Crowe, 8

...it means that they are my friend and they trust me.
Schuyler Yedlin, 8

...I'll do good favors for them and be nice to them most of the time.
Max Goodley, 8

...I take care of them—so if someone got hurt, I would get them an ice pack.
Liesel Staubitz, 6

Love is the kind of thing you like to do with your mom and dad and friends that you really love a lot. When you love someone you hug and kiss them.

Quincy Engelbrecht, 7

You show people you love them by giving them all your love and care. You read them stories and you kiss them.

Eleanor Silverstein, 9

Love is when somebody loves you. My mom loves me. She hugs me. I kiss her. I love my dad. I kiss him.

Abbie Benford, 5

I don't know much about love, but I love my friend Forrest. I hug him.

Cole McCann-Phillips, 3

You could hug someone to let them know you love them. My mom kisses me when I get on the bus.

Caleb Mahoney, 6

My dad hugs me, my mom kisses me, my sisters hug and kiss me.

Connor Barnett, 8

Love makes me want to hug my mommy and daddy, because I love them very much. I also love my cat Midnight, except she's a little bit pouncey—she pounces everywhere.

Lilly Barnett, 7

I hug and kiss the people I love. People who love me care about me and they help me.

Tifton Medicinehorse, 11

LOVE means

God makes you

hug each other.

Gabriel Newbrun-Mintz, 2

I can tell I love someone when I take care of them and when I hold them…and…I can just tell. I can feel love in my heart. It's kind of calm and really…sort of…I feel really really good.

Leah Grillo, 8

It feels weird, but a good kind of weird.

Alon Sacks, 9

I think you should love people for who they are, and not for who they aren't.

Sophie Gilchrist, 11

I feel love in my heart; it feels weird, but a good kind of weird.

Love is a feeling that makes you feel safe. When you love someone, your heart brights up.

Mallory Bragg, 8

Love makes me feel good, and safe.

Matthew Schabel, 7

Love is when you care for someone and if they're hurt you help them.

Aaron Smith, 9

Love is when you like someone
so much more than anything.
It is greater than
great. If you love someone
so much sometimes you kiss them
and hug them. If you are a grown-up
you could marry them.
Love makes you feel so good in
your heart.

Madison Naomi Schobinger, 6

Love means peace,
understanding, and
caring.

Anji Herman, 10

Love is light.
Love makes me feel happy.
Love is a toy store.

Theo Chamberlain, 3

...they help me with problems at school and with life. They get me what I need to succeed; they give me encouragement. My dad pushes me to succeed. He pushed me to get my black belt in karate. He helped me get on the soccer team in school. My mom does the same things for me. Love makes you feel good.

Danny Sacks, 11

...they help me with homework and take me on vacations because they want me to see other places.

Lauren Christianson, 10

...Mom and Dad say they love me all of the time, and they buy me presents and take me to fun places. If they didn't love me they would just leave me out and wouldn't play with me.

Zoe Goldberg, 6

...my mom cares about me and she takes care of me and so does my dad—they give me what I really need.

Elena Bakar, 8

...Daddy kisses and hugs me and tells me he loves me when he wakes me up.

Madison Naomi Schobinger, 6

...they let me have my friends over all the time. They give me a lot of attention. They always have time to listen to something I have to say.

Leah Grillo, 8

...my dad plays with me. If you didn't love your son, you wouldn't play with your son.

Elliott Stone, 12

...my mommy takes us to the pool. She takes us to the park. We play on the swings. My mommy reads me books. It feels nice.

Sophia Simon, 4

...ove me because...
know my parents love me because...
cause...I know my parents love me because

...my mom loves me because she gives me breakfast: my favorite is when she makes me strudel with icing.

Matthew Schabel, 7

...they say they love me on my birthday. They take care of me. They help me with my homework. They teach me stuff. They send me to camp. I couldn't go to camp without them, because they have to figure it all out. They give me a home. I could go on and on here.

Alexandra Goldstein, 10

...they do really good things for me like help me learn new things like homework. My mom teaches me new recipes that she learned from her mom. They hug me and tuck me in at night, care for me a lot, and cheer me up when I'm sad. They take me to my games and cheer me on at soccer, basketball, and softball. Love feels great.

Kaylie Kathleen Williams, 10.

...my mama gets things down for me that I can't reach. She looks for things that I lost.

Katherine Mary Scotnicki, 5

...because Mom tells me she does. She sings me to sleep and she does hand massage.

Tyler Briant Nierstedt, 6

...they help me with my homework and by telling me they love me and by tucking me into bed at night.

Justin Jones, 11

...they hug and kiss me and protect me.

Tyler Mahoney, 4

Mommy loves me 'cause she likes me and wants me to get healthy and strong. Daddy loves me, he likes me and he's happy, 'cause his grandparents and his mom love each other and loved him when he was a little boy and a big boy and when he was a teenager. Animals love me but they don't hurt me; they like me 'cause I'm nice to them, 'cause they love me back—they give me kisses, they lick me. Even Stormy licks me.

Malia Kristina Bertelsen, 4

I love Mama and she loves me. I like to make pictures for my mom and tell her she can take them to work, so they remind her of me. Love is like when you make a heart, it kind of reminds me of love. People should make a card that says **I Love You.**

Katherine Mary Scotnicki, 5

Love is joy and happiness and good feelings about someone. If someone's nice to you, if they're kind and help you, then you know they love you.

Karl Bach, 11

I tell my parents I love them. I also help them with a lot, like I clean my room so they don't have to do it. As I get older, I do more and more stuff like chores and things like that, and that really helps them—so that's a way of showing that I love them.

Alexandra Goldstein, 10

I feel love in my heart. Love is a feeling that could hurt or feel great. Love could hurt because you could find out the person or thing you love doesn't love you back or doesn't exist. Love could feel great if a person you love would love you back or exist.

Kylee Larsen, 12

I feel love when I'm at home doing things with my family.

Lauren Christianson, 10

Love is something inside.
It's a strong feeling that
makes you show kindness
to people and nature.

Elena Scott, 12

Love is fabulous because
it feels good. It feels good to
be loved and to love.
Love is caring and sharing
and giving everything
that matters to other people.
When you love, it is fun
every day; and when you are
loved you feel protected
and important. You can love
a lot of people in different
ways, but it is all love if you
care and share.

Lauren Moscarello, 8

Love is an extremely close relationship, and it's
full of different emotions about someone else.
People show love physically by kissing, and
verbally when they talk. You can also tell by
the way they look at each other and the way
they act around each other.

Justin Jones, 11

Love is nice. I usually feel love in my heart. It
feels good just to know that somebody loves
me and that they'll take care of me. Say you
love your parents; you can get in an argument,
but you still love each other because you're
family. I like it when my parents come to my
performances. It makes me feel really good to
see my parents in the audience.

Danielle Schatzman, 8

If I think about who I love, I feel something
inside. There's a feeling that tells me, like
someone is inside me, sort of like the real me
is inside me, keeping track of everything,
reminding me of what everything is.

Cole Page, 12

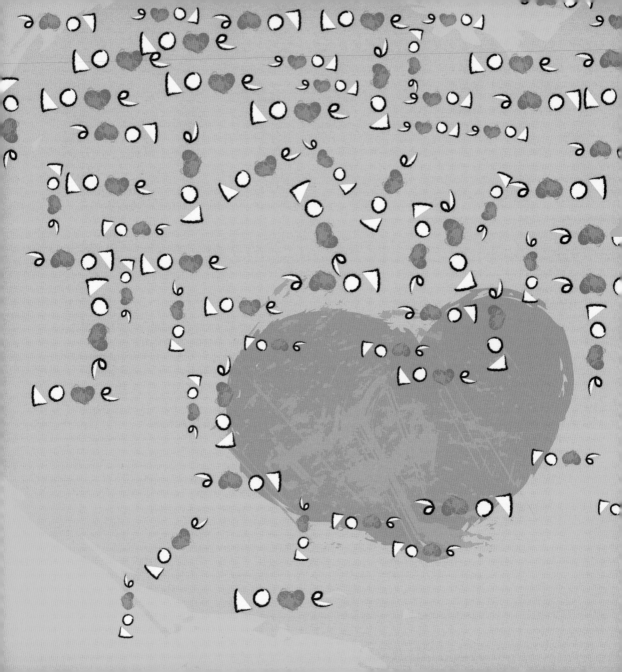

Love is when someone has a passion for someone else, when they feel happy together.

Jill Meserve, 11

I feel love in my tummy.

Zoe Goldberg, 6

Love is something that we think, we feel, we do. People who love you give you hugs and support you every day and they look out for you; that's how you know they love you—they help you through hard times and they urge you on when you think you're doing something you can't do. They're just always there for you.

TJ Dempsey, 11

Love is something you can only feel if it's what's supposed to happen. It's a tingly feeling that's hard to explain. When you're deeply thinking about someone you love, you can't help but smile deeply. You should behave in the kindest manner possible towards the ones you love. Nature is a very easy thing to love, because of all the risks you can take, like climbing a mountain or to the top of a tree or looking in a volcano.

Lilah Clevey, 11

Love is a feeling. It's different for every person, and you feel it differently with every person you meet. What makes love *love* is that it's a feeling you can't describe. You can describe your anger but you can't really describe love. You know it's there but you can't really touch it; it's in air.

Angelique Traub, 12

Love would be when you really really care for someone and you do a lot for them and you wouldn't forget about them and you care for them almost more than you would care for yourself.

Cortnay Cymrot, 10

People who love me make sure I don't go running in the streets, because they care about me. I feel love in my whole body, in my heart…I don't feel my heart booming when it happens, it's just kind of throughout me.

Chelsea Cymrot, 12

I love God because he made us.

Aaron Stone, 8

When someone from my family says "I love you," it makes me feel good and makes me feel that someone is there for me. Other love, between boys and girls not in the same family, is different. That love is kind of tickly—a little more embarrassing. It's way different.

Elliott Stone, 12

It's good to hug people. It's important to tell people "I love you." I love you as much as the sky stays!

Anya Rauchle, 6

Love is respecting and being kind to others. I love you to the stars and back!

Alex Rauchle, 7

Love is caringness, to be helpful, to show kindness to other people.

Ari Bental, 9

I feel love in my heart.
It feels good to have somebody
that loves me and cares for me.
I love animals; if you love them
they love you. It's good to have
animals because if you had a
bad day you could just go
cuddle up with them and tell
them all that's happening, and
you'll feel like somebody's
really listening.
Carrie Brandon, 9

When people are nice to you,
I'm really happy.
Sophia Simon, 4

Love is when you like
someone a lot, and you play
with them and talk with them.
Love feels good. I love my
mom. I hug her. I talk with her
and read a book with her. I love
my dog and cat and I feed
them and pet them. We should
love animals.
Lucia Simon, 6

Love is a strong mutual
bond and respect between two
or more people, or it could
even be between an object and
a person; but that would have
to be very strong for that
to be love.
Eric Brandon, 13

Love is something where
you hug people and kiss
people. I feel love in my heart.
Alexander Palmer, 5

Love is compassion between
two people. Love feels
emotional. People are kind to
you and tell you they love you.
They try to make you happy.
Spencer Palmer, 10

Being with children is *love*.

Children are filled with light from the heavens.

Being with a child is feeling *love* all around.

Love feels like a radiation, or a golden fluid,

like when it's raining;

it's like golden drops filling your body.

Love is a simple thing;

it's a pure **warmth** that fills our body.

Zoe Loughran Brezsny, 12

Love is quiet. If people get sick in the belly, I help them.
Taylor Childers, 5

If you love someone, you take care of them. And if someone loves you, they take care of you. When someone loves me, I feel it in my tummy. I feel married.
Nicole Childers, 5

Love is a really really really strong bond between people.
Claire Lipsman, 8

Love is a good feeling: it's having someone you can talk to, and that you know loves you.
Evan Steinbaum, 12

Love is when a parent tries to comfort their kid when they are upset. When someone loves you, you know they will care for you. I am nice to the people I love, and I try to make them feel good about something they didn't do good at.
Lauren Steinbaum, 12

Love is peace. Love makes me feel happy, it makes me feel that someone knows me and loves me. When you love someone, you hug them, be nice to them, and buy them presents.
Benny Bakar, 8

I know someone loves me because I can see it by their feeling. Love is nice.
Elena Bakar, 8

I feel love in my heart. It is a
warm feeling inside. I love my
parents and they love me. They
love me because I'm their child.
I draw pictures for them.
Sometimes I give them candy.
Molly McCann, 10

Everyone has love, look inside.
Everybody has it. It's a feeling.
Some people don't use it
but they could if they wanted
to. Use love every day to help
the world out.
Sarah Wiener, 13

Use love every day to help the world out.

Love is when you really like
someone and you're friends
with him or her. They say
"I love you" and give you stuff,
like heart candy or roses.
Kylee Koenig, 12

Love is passion and giving and
hugging. Spreading peace in the
world is love. Being nice to
people is love.
Haley Pacheco, 11

Love is something very special. You can see love anywhere, really, if you look for it, like a rose opening. People have love in their hearts. People who love you are kind and they always make sure you feel good. I am kind back to them, I appreciate them, and I do things that show them that I love them. Sometimes I go out into the garden and pick a bouquet of flowers for them.

Elsinore Smidth, 13

Love is happy!

Jacqueline Norton, 3

Love is caring for someone,

and caring about

their health.

Stewart Gruen, 11

Love is pretty hard to explain. I feel love in my mind and my heart. I love my parents and my cat. I tell them I love them and I hang out with them. I hang out with my cat during the day. I pet her a lot and I give her treats. She likes me for that. I know people love me when they talk to me about stuff and help me solve problems.

Evan Cranston, 9

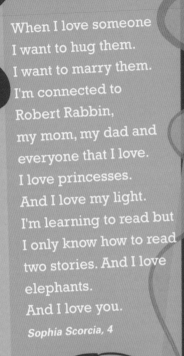

When I love someone
I want to hug them.
I want to marry them.
I'm connected to
Robert Rabbin,
my mom, my dad and
everyone that I love.
I love princesses.
And I love my light.
I'm learning to read but
I only know how to read
two stories. And I love
elephants.
And I love you.

Sophia Scorcia, 4

When somebody borns you it means they love you because it is your baby.

Lucy Black, 6

Love means
you love people.
I feel love
under a rainbow.
I've seen a real
rainbow before.
I remember
two of the colors,
red and orange.
Angels make you
have magic.

Tyler Mahoney, 4

Love is when two people are nice to each other. Love is also like in nature—like I love animals. And when you love things, you take care of them.

Cali Slepin, 8

Loving is caring for people and things—a dog, or a bird. Happiness is to do things for other people; when you do, it makes you feel good and it makes them feel good.

Emma Rubinowitz, 11

I love animals. I like their sounds—how they run. The animals are special to me. When animals get shot, I get really sad.

Mallory Bragg, 8

Love is when you look in someone's eyes and they really smile

Robert Lehmann, 9

Love is when you like someone
a lot, a lot, a lot!

Good night, Mommy, I love you.

I love you all the way down to

the bottom of the ocean and then back up!

I love you all the way to

heaven and back

and that's a long way!

Zane Schobinger, 4

love

   sweet and pure

      like a bird flying

             to its freedom

                 love longs to wrap

                   its golden arms around you

       two heads rested together

      two hands softly clenched

        love

  like a stream clasping

       to its bed of moss

             and a summer day

               lingering in the sky

         a child runs into a mother's soft caress

     and love opens its eyes even wider to the world

Zoe Loughran Brezsny, 12

"Peace is not really one thing," says Siena Hood, "it's an all around atmosphere." Lilah Clevey tells us "peace is happiness." It is "quiet and beautiful and colorful," says Kaylie Kathleen Williams. Robert Lehmann teaches us "peace is freedom." Kylee Larsen knows "peace is friendship among people." Then Aaron Smith hits the bull's-eye: "Peace is the total opposite of war." And Mabel Herrick backs him up: "War is not good."

This was their mantra, this was their chant. Over and over, they said, "No War. NO WAR." The very idea of war is shocking to them; as a means to solve problems it is "pathetic" and "insane."

And yet to us, these kids are not "anti-war"; they are not standing on the opposite side of "pro-war." They are standing on higher ground. They are standing on the summit of love, on the pure peak of connection and oneness with all living things. From this summit, they say: **War is not good. Don't do it. Find another way.**

When Cole Page says "peace is a unity with everyone," he suggests that peace is the expression of God. If God is the unity of all things, and if love is the feeling of unity, then peace is the expression of unity. We all belong to the same family. We love our brothers and sisters. We don't hurt the people we love.

Give peace a chance. Amen.

Peace is when everyone is *getting along* in the whole world.

People need to respect everyone that lives.

Elliott Stone, 12

PEA

I think we need a bigger piece o

Angelique Traub,

Peace would be when everyone is free.

Caleb Mahoney, 6

ICE

peace

Peace can be as simple as a flower. It's not really one thing. It's an all around atmosphere.

Siena Hood, 12

Peace

...when there are no problems happening around you.

Jill Meserve, 11

...freedom and the right to do what you want to do and stand up for your rights. People should have their heads straight and not try to be mean to other countries just because they have different rules than you. Try to stay away from war.

Robert Lehmann, 9

...not like anything that's harmful; it's totally the opposite. You don't feel like you're in danger. And it's comfortable.

Molly McCann, 10

...being free. If you have peace you get along with everyone and share your life with everyone. In the world if there is peace there are no wars and no one has to die fighting. If you have peace it is easy to love because everyone is thinking about everyone else and love is what brings you together.

Lauren Moscarello, 8

...when there is nothing wrong, and there is no fighting or war.

Jeremiah Byers, 12

...the total opposite of war.

Aaron Smith, 9

...to treat people how you want to be treated.

Afton Wight, 8

...when you're cool and happy.

Kylee Koenig, 12

...friendship among people, or silence.

Kylee Larsen, 12

...no war; everybody is loving each other.

Spencer Palmer, 10

The image of peace would be a yin-yang sign, of course, or a peace sign. But peace itself is happiness—everyone working together, teamwork. I think that war as a way to solve problems is really pathetic. You can't solve a problem by creating more problems. You have to find a way that is peaceful. It's like fighting off a mosquito with a bigger mosquito. Usually a problem is between two people, two leaders. Why should the leaders pull in all the innocent families? The two leaders should get together and solve their own problems without involving other people.

Lilah Clevey, 11

I think peace means "stop" because my friend Denver held up two fingers to the cars on the street. I think he wanted them to stop. A war is when people fight. I don't know why they fight. They shouldn't fight. They should be nice to each other.

Zane Schobinger, 4

Peace is the medicine.

Albert Brown, 8

What if war weren't an option?

Peace is just everybody being together and not being mean to each other, getting along. I would have a meeting with a bunch of people from all over the world, and I'd tell them to compromise. I'd say, "Okay, we just don't go to war, we just try to settle things in a different way. We don't need war. It's just killing more people." We could try to agree with each other and listen to each other, to other people's recommendations, and listen. Even if you don't agree, don't cut them off, just listen. Then when it's your turn, you can tell them.

Carrie Brandon, 9

Peace is quiet and everyone likes each other. People don't hit each other or be mean to each other. They do not fight or hit someone with a real sword. If I was the Queen I would tell everyone to be nice and don't be mean to each other. Don't fight and don't have wars. Play Barbies and ponies with each other instead.

Madison Naomi Schobinger, 6

The war is going right now. It makes me mad. They're shooting guns and people are getting run over. We should do peace-rallying.

Cole McCann-Phillips, 3

War is like a disease, and it won't go away until you take the right medication.

Marshall Levensohn, 9

The key to peace is to unite in friendship rather than on the battlefield with an M16 in your hands. For peace, we have to just be nice to other people, races, and nations. We have to learn to let strong emotions come without acting upon them. I'd like to emphasize that war doesn't decide who is right: it just decides who is left.

Miles Ceralde, 12

Peace means that
you have to not argue
and that you should
be nice to each other
and be friends with each other;
actually you don't have to be friends,
but just...Don't argue

Respect one another
No weapons
No fighting
No war...

Danielle Schatzman, 8

War is scary. I wouldn't want to be in the middle of it. If I had kids I wouldn't want them to grow up in warfare.

Ariel Filane, 12

Peace means no war, no war at all. I think peace is anything that resolves a fight, anything that you can do to resolve something that is going on in your life.

Julia Egger, 13

Peace means no wars, don't fight—have a piece of life.

Quincy Engelbrecht, 7

Peace is when no one fights, and there's no chemicals or bombs or stuff that hurts people.

Luke Garrison, 13

If we went to war, it wouldn't be good for Mother Earth. We'd be killing everything alive.

Adrian Franco, 11

Keep the peace. Do not make wars. There is no good reason for wars.

Eden Knodel, 8

Lots of people when they think of peace they
think of war and war stopping, but even
if there was no war in the world right now we'd
still have poverty and people who are the
rich people who don't really think of the poor
people as the same people as they are.
Peace is more of a unity with everyone, with
everyone being mostly equal. When I think of
peace, I think of everyone sharing everything
they have, and I think of unlocked doors and
everyone trusting everyone. It's just like
everyone is united.

Cole Page, 12

If we lived in a peaceful world, I'm not sure
anyone would have made up the game of
football or hockey. If we lived in a peaceful
world, people would be nice to each other,
they wouldn't get into fights or rob other
people or try to take over the world.

Justin Jones, 11

When you're peaceful,
you are nice and friendly.

Taylor Childers, 5

Nicole Childers, 5

Peace means quiet. Peace is like everyone is quiet; like if you have a class you can say that my class was peaceful, because they didn't say much.

Katherine Mary Scotnicki, 5

Don't fight with people because if it starts in your family it will spread. Start being peaceful first, and then help the world.

Sarah Wiener, 13

Peace and understanding are the important things to keep in mind. Stop the wars and have less violence. War is a stupid idea. If people have to settle something, they can talk about it.

Anji Herman, 10

Peace is when everyone likes each other and they're being nice to each other, there is no war, and everything is calm and mellow. I had a nightmare: it was like I was in Afghanistan instead of America, and suddenly they started bombing. There were all these bombs coming down, and it was really noisy and scary and all these kids are jumping into bushes. That was pretty scary to me. To not have wars, the first thing I would say is to get a president who doesn't want to have wars. You know what happened on September 11? Well, they did that to us, so if we go to war with them, it will just make more of the same thing, and that is a bad idea. There isn't much more to say except that war wouldn't be good and peace would be a great thing. God might be able to help, and love might be able to help. Who knows?

Evan Cranston, 9

Peace means nobody is getting hurt; nobody is getting hurt and going to the hospital. That's what peace means to me.
Zoe Goldberg, 6

Peace means that everybody isn't always arguing or fighting, or having wars and people being shot; it's just nice and calm and everybody is getting along. I feel pretty bad when it isn't peaceful. When things are peaceful, I don't have to be worrying a whole lot, because I know everybody is safe.
Leah Grillo, 8

Peace means you shouldn't bother people and it means to be nice. Like these days they're saying "Peace on Earth" because we're having war, so they don't want war, so they're saying "be nice" so we won't have wars.
Elena Bakar, 8

Peace is when there is no war and everyone is nice to each other.
Lila Hood, 8

I think peace is where no one hates each other and where no one is against each other. But I don't think that can happen.
Karl Bach, 11

War is bad 'cause people can get hurt, and it's not very nice to kill people.
Benny Bakar, 8

I think peace should be a part of our lives; it's a simple way of having your life be a good life, by being peaceful. Everyone has some peacefulness in them, but I guess that some people need to find it. We have to make sure we show the peace we have inside.
Elsinore Smidth, 13

Peace is no fighting, everybody is happy, everybody is content, nothing bad is happening to each country. No one fights.
Alexandra Goldstein, 10

Peace means to not fight and be happy with everyone else.
Ari Bental, 9

I wouldn't start a war. Fighting is not love. Be loving and kind.
Mattias Hanson, 10

Peace means that you have a lot of joy. A peaceful place really means there is nothing that's bad about it. It's very calm.
Tyler Briant Nierstedt, 6

We should learn to share. For example, in the war over Jerusalem—a holy place for Muslims, Christians, and Jews— there's all these wars revolving around it. There would be so many fewer wars and there'd be many more lives right now if people would just learn to share. I would like to stop all the wars as much as possible.
Eric Brandon, 13

You should use your words instead of fighting; you should talk things out. If someone was being mean and made someone cry, I would tell them to say they are sorry. I don't give put-downs or make fun of someone.
Mallory Bragg, 8

Peace should be between everyone. If people are being mean, they are just trying to work out their anger. We should try to bring peace instead of anger into the world.

Amanda Slaughter, 10

I feel peace is good. It's nice for other people to have peace and quiet. It's very nice for people to love each other.

Joshua Slaughter, 8

I think peace is a thing that people really like, because it's quiet. I like peace.

Lilly Barnett, 7

Peace is quietness. It's not about war. It's having fun with your family. Peace is just peace. I would try to bring peace.

Connor Barnett, 8

Peace is when there are no arguments between people or nations. There are no problems between people. You can be nicer to more people and not try to hurt people.

Danny Sacks, 11

Peace means not harming anything and being nice and trying to make friends, buying them food or giving them a flower.

Alon Sacks, 9

Peace is having no wars. Peace is calm. Peace is no violence. Listen to other people when they're talking. Don't compete, because that makes people fight.

Thomas Medicinehorse, 12

Peace means to leave people alone.

Tifton Medicinehorse, 11

I think that war is stupid. Even if you try not to kill innocent people, in a war you probably would.

Lauren Steinbaum, 12

Peace is no fighting; it's just calm. Fighting is not a good way to solve problems. It's better to talk things out.

Evan Steinbaum, 12

Peace is when you're quiet,
even with someone else.

Marcus Christianson, 6

Peace is when nobody
fights and everybody
gets along.

Lauren Christianson, 10

The most important thing in life is life, being alive. Life is a gift from God and he gave you the opportunity to live. You shouldn't waste it on war and killing each other. Don't kill each other. I don't see the reason to do that. If there is a reason to kill, I haven't seen it. I hope that there will be all peace.

Ben Herrick, 11

Peace is when basically two countries depend on each other and have lots of friendship; no peace is when there's war. Peace is when you're friends, when you get along with someone. You don't have to like the person, but you should still be nice to them and include them.

Chelsea Cymrot, 12

War is not good; it makes a lot of people die and it is about something pointless. I don't want to go to war. I don't want to be killed that way. Talk it out.

Mabel Herrick, 7

Peace feels like nothing bad going on, no war, no pollution—no anything bad going on. Peace is just like some invention that makes everything work right. I don't know what it would be.

Cortnay Cymrot, 10

Peace is when the whole country comes together.

We wouldn't have racism.

Peace is definitely a piece of what's going on in the world. I think we need a bigger piece of peace. Like cake, once you start eating it, it's hard to get off the chocolate. Peace gives you more self-confidence.

Angelique Traub, 12

There is rarely any peace for me in my house living with my 2-year-old brother Gabriel.

Eli Newbrun-Mintz, 7

The important things in life are to keep peace and to remember your family—to be kind to them, to take care of them, and to be nice to them.

Cali Slepin, 8

Peace makes everything better. Even if you are under attack during a war and it doesn't look very bright, even still try to make things better, don't just give up and start to destroy things and get really angry. You could make a sign for peace, or a poem. Never lose hope. Try to be as strong as you can, even if it's really hard. Try to make things better for people who will come after you.

Ciro Podany, 12

It is pointless to fight. It just destroys a whole lot of people. Work things out together; figure it out.

Nadia Herman, 10

War is a combination of hatred and frustration. There should be a better way to resolve things. The things that I see on TV—bombs exploding—we shouldn't see these things, they shouldn't be happening, and just because it's not happening in San Francisco doesn't mean it isn't happening. Like Martin Luther King said, you cannot defeat hatred with hatred, you must defeat it with love. A year without war would be a major victory for the world.

Terry Castleman, 9

Peace means that everybody is getting along and not giving each other a hard time (but if it's just teasing it's okay). And everybody kind of loving each other and caring for each other and not making everybody else mad. It's like Martin Luther King, Jr. said: everybody can be the same; they can do the same things so they are evenly fit. He said that everybody should be able to love and do the same things and have the same rights.

TJ Dempsey, 11

Peace makes you feel like you can do anything you want. You can go buy food. You don't have people who say *go do this* and *go do that*; it's like freedom.

Aaron Stone, 8

I don't think anyone likes war, except people who are insane. I think a way of solving a problem is like a tennis game or a soccer game.

Alex Leason, 12

We'd all be one people.

Lucinda Watson, 12

Please remember the children of the dawning day

Do not let your anger dirty the waters of people's dreams

Give the world a future with no wrong way

Decide to dance a life that will say

Happiness and love, a life that gleams

Please remember the children of the dawning day

Joy was never meant to fade away

Let your life smile a smile that beams

Give the world a future with no wrong way

Peace is a song that must play

With radiance and without one broken seam

Please remember the children of the dawning day

Give the world a future with no wrong way.

Elsinore Smidth, 13

God is the unity of all things, love is the feeling of unity,
and peace is the expression of unity. This is the natural order of
things. But we have lost touch with this and have fallen on
hard times.

We have to heal ourselves back into harmony with life.
The kids know how and these are their specific and precise
recommendations. Get ready to take notes. There is a lot
of work to do.

Some kids offer advice on parenting, others talk about wanting
to teach children. Some share their sadness at our treatment of
animals and mourn the loss of their habitats. Many ask us
to stop littering, polluting, and desecrating Mother Earth. They
want all people to have food, shelter, and clothing. We are
reminded to move slowly through life and to appreciate each
moment, because life is short. Be kind and do good deeds.
Respect and help each other. Get rid of all weapons. Distribute
wealth. Develop compassion. Make sure *everyone* is safe.

DON'T CUT DOWN TREES. They were so adamant about
this that we decided to print this book on paper made from
sugar cane pulp.

There is a lot of suffering in this world. It is not too late to
make a new life for ourselves and for our world, one in which
the natural order of life is respected.

Here are the instructions. Read carefully and follow exactly.

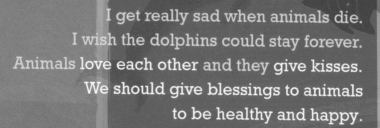

I get really sad when animals die.
I wish the dolphins could stay forever.
Animals love each other and they give kisses.
We should give blessings to animals
to be healthy and happy.

Isabel Rauchle, 3

HEA

People should stop cutting down trees and killing animals for pleasure.

Be yourself. Don't try to be someone else.

Mabel Herrick, 7

stead of making war, I would have a championship
nnis game between people who disagree.
ar kills and I hate the idea of killing.
eople should be more patient and caring with kids.

Michelle Leason, 10

LING

Respect everything. Respect the Earth.
Be helpful for one another. Be courteous,
kind, truthful. Don't be harming animals.
Don't kill anybody else.
Treat people good and they'll treat you good.

Thomas Medicinehorse, 12

I think that we should think of things as they really are; like rocks: people just look at them and say, "Oh, just another rock." But if you really think about it, rocks are a lot. We should take everything for what it really is, not take anything for granted. We should treat animals a lot differently than we do now. We should not unnecessarily kill any animals inhumanely. I wouldn't like to be slaughtered inhumanely. I would like to be fed right, to have a nice habitat or environment. I wouldn't like to be caged up like in some zoos; I wouldn't like to be in a circus tamed by lion-tamers. I think that's extremely cruel: big magnificent beasts being trained to jump through a hoop. It's just not right.

Eric Brandon, 13

There is a lot of trash thrown everywhere, so we should recycle more and re-use things more than we do now.
Danny Sacks, 11

The world would be a better place if people stopped using so much paper.
Eli Newbrun-Mintz, 7

Mother Earth is basically the trees: if you chop them down, then that's like chopping one of her arms off. Mother Earth would have lots of arms if all the trees were her arms, so you shouldn't chop them off, because it hurts. If you cut down the trees it's like cutting your arms off. Don't litter or spit on the ground. I try to tell my friends not to do that. Littering is bad for the Earth; animals could come around and say, "Yum food." But litter is bad for them—once they eat it, they choke and die. And then they'll become extinct, so there's not much left of those animals—and don't shoot them. If you shoot them, they die, and then there's none of them left if you keep on shooting them.

Connor Barnett, 8

People shouldn't do graffiti because the people who do are just trying to be rude and they think they're cool doing it; and they just don't have a life, so they say, "What the heck, let's just do this."
Ari Bental, 9

We should be respectful of the environment. Without trees we cannot live. God made them. If we destroy them, they won't come back very fast.
Elliott Stone, 12

We should behave respectfully towards nature; tend the Earth with kindness, because it gives us so much. I had a pet mouse. It's the only animal I ever had. Instead of getting a rambunctious dog, I got this small gray mouse. I had to be so gentle and careful with it. Animals can teach us in this way—how to be more tender and gentle.
Zoe Loughran Brezsny, 12

I know that Mother Earth goes to sleep in winter and wakes up in spring. We should respect the animals. We should not cut down a lot of the forest and only use a little of the lumber; only take as much as you need. And the same with the plants: only take as much as you need especially if the animals eat those plants—like cabbage and carrots. People should not litter the Earth.
Tyler Briant Nierstedt, 6

When I'm grown up, the grown-ups now will be grandmas and grandpas. The grown-ups need to clean the world and pick up leaves in the park. They have to pick up the litter that people drop on the ground like pop cans.
Madison Naomi Schobinger, 6

Trees help you live, they give you oxygen, so we should take care of them, don't cut them down, feed them. We should treat animals nicely; don't hunt them—feed them, care for them.
Benny Bakar, 8

If you love the Earth, you'd be going in the opposite direction of pretty much every government right now. The world could be prospering if they had love. The government right now is ruining everything. In 100 years, the kids living then, I don't think there's going to be anything nice. It's going downhill now.
Ciro Podany, 12

Grown-ups are sometimes a little bit stuck up about their beliefs and I think they should give kids more responsibility. Just because we're younger doesn't mean we don't know stuff. There's definitely stuff that kids see that grown-ups are blind to it. So I think adults should listen to kids.
Siena Hood, 12

Maybe adults should actually listen to our ideas instead of disregarding them. I think some governments should listen to its people more, considering a government is its people.

Stewart Gruen, 11

When adults tell kids not to do something, they shouldn't do those things themselves. We should all respect each other, no matter where you are.
Learn to respect others and be non-harming, and don't argue about religions. If you hurt someone's feelings, you want to make sure you apologize to them because it will make them feel better. It is important to always be loving and kind to others.
Alex Rauchle, 7

People might look mean on the outside, but they have a good heart. We should look for the goodness in people's heart.
I had the idea to pick flowers from my mom's garden and sell them at Whole Foods, and then give the money to poor people, so they could have a place to live and something to eat.

Mallory Bragg, 8

Sometimes adults really misunderstand kids; they think, "Oh, they're kids and they don't know anything." Adults should listen more to children; it would make it easier for us to be kids. Wherever you are in the world, if you get scared and think, "Oh no, nobody loves me," there is always someone who loves you.
Lucinda Watson, 12

I think we should be respectful to other people around the world, not just people of your same religion or nation. I think everyone in the whole world should be free. I think we can be nice to everyone from a different country who comes into our country. We need to give them support.
Elliott Stone, 12

When grown-ups say things, it mostly goes because kids don't exactly have that much power. When you grow up and become an adult you sort of lose your kid, and you turn into your parents, or someone who's more of the boss over the kids. It would be cool if when we grew up, we remembered everything about being a kid and made it easier to be a kid. A great life for me would be if everyone around me was happy and equal. It would be better if everyone around me had a good life.

Cole Page, 12

The world would be a better place with **no drugs** and more **recycling**.

Tifton Medicinehorse, 11

Don't hurt your **kids**, and be **happy.**

Kylee Koenig, 12

I think it's really important that people live their lives calmly and not try to harm or hurt someone else. To live calmly is to be centered and focused and present where you are and not dwelling on a certain emotion that could harm others. Meditation helps you stay present, not daydreaming, noticing what's going on around you. It helps because it opens up your heart to other people.

Miles Ceralde, 12

Just because someone is different doesn't mean they're bad. Just because a lot of people think they know something, it doesn't mean it is. Animals teach us lessons. They are smarter than us. You don't see a whole lot of animals fighting over one thing; we can learn from them. Big factories have a lot of pollution. When I grow up the whole world might be full of pollution and I won't be able to breathe.

Nadia Herman, 10

I want to unite the world. I just don't understand racism and things like that. We are all the same and we all are one. We are different in tiny little ways and somehow that makes some people hate other people who seem different. Try and love someone who you don't. My sister went to Hawaii and the schools were on strike and a lot of kids were starving because the only way they got food was from their schools and so I want to gather money together and get food for those children.
Sarah Wiener, 13

I think what adults should do is any child who doesn't have a home or a family, they should try to find somebody to take care of them or a home for them to stay in.
Lila Hood, 8

Healing is where you help people. I'm trying to heal Grandma. I touch her and I try healing her. She says it's making her feel better. She needs it. It's very hard for her to do things. It's very nice for people to love each other.
Joshua Slaughter, 8

I want to help children. Children have to know that there is hope for them. Someone cares for them and loves them, even if they don't see it.
Julia Egger, 13

The best way to have a good life is to do what you want to and not feel like you have to do what someone else says you should do. Just do what you want to. Be yourself.
Evan Steinbaum, 12

The Indians used to say there is a wheel in your stomach and it has **sharp ends,** and when you lie it turns and **pokes** you and makes you **feel bad**. If you **keep lying,** finally the ends will **wear off** and you can't **feel** it anymore—**you can't even feel the bad things you do to other people** because you've lied so much.

Emma Rubinowitz, 11

If you do things to destroy your body, like eat unhealthy foods or smoke tobacco or drink too much alcohol or don't exercise, you're just going to make it worse on yourself. Always leave a moment for yourself; never be in too much of a rush. Rich people should give money to the poor; just because they made all that money doesn't mean they should keep it to themselves.
Lilah Clevey, 11

on't be mean to people who don't look like you.
Caleb Mahoney, 6

If you work hard and are determined to make your life better, it will get better.
Lauren Steinbaum, 12

Generosity is important, which is giving money to people who don't have money. You don't need money to live a good life, but you do need a home.
Anji Herman, 10

Dare to be different. My dad said that to me once in a speech competition. I was doing impromptu, where you make it up on the spot, and he says, "Dare to be different." I think that's a lot like life, because in life you have no idea what's going to happen. You cannot be afraid to go out and do something. If you sit back and are afraid—"Oh, should I do this?"—you'll never get anywhere in life.
Eric Brandon, 13

It's important to have fun while you're a kid. Education and health are very important also. More people should exercise more regularly. It is very important to exercise.
Alex Leason, 12

If my friend was sick I'd write them a note and send them a present to make them feel better. If one of my friends were getting picked on, I would stand up for them.
Jacob Dorfman, 8

If you don't take care of Mother Earth, she could punish you with her animals. Keep her animals safe, keep the Earth beautiful, don't cut down too many trees, and use natural stuff—don't use stuff that makes the world icky with pollution. I think that since God was your creator you should take care of his place.
Cali Slepin, 8

My favorite animal is the red wolf. They are an endangered species and I would like to respect them a little bit more. Don't hunt them and don't kill the surroundings around them so they don't die as much.
Kaylie Kathleen Williams, 10

I like all animals. I don't think people should throw their trash outside the window because animals might not be able to eat that stuff, even though they'll try to. I love horses and cats and dogs and hamsters and guinea pigs. I like all animals. I like baby pigs. I love babies, too. We should make boats with extra metal, so they won't leak oil and kill fish and birds.
Michelle Leason, 10

We should cut down less forests, because I really like animals and the loss of habitats can cause extinction of animals. Also, trees provide oxygen, and we breathe in oxygen. So, cut down less forests.
Rachel Knodel, 11

My favorite animals are African animals: cheetahs and lions and leopards. I'm going to go to Africa when I'm either 22 or 21 and tell them to stop poaching those animals so people can go to the camps down there to look at the animals.
Marcus Christianson, 6

My favorite animal is the deer.
We should feed them.
Abbie Benford, 5

I have three animals: a leopard, a cheetah,
and a dog. I feed them and give them water.
Alexander Palmer, 5

We should treat animals like they're another
person, a person that you love.
Jill Meserve, 11

We should care for animals. The only time
you should ever dissect an animal is if it has a
disease, so you can learn from it.
Alex Leason, 12

My favorite animals are the elephants. We
shouldn't capture them. We should leave them
free.
Caleb Mahoney, 6

To show animals you love them, you could give
them food. You could find a nest of a bird and
give them food so when the birds flew back
they could eat it.
Katherine Mary Scotnicki, 5

Some animals are dying and we want to take
care of them. Take care of animals, feed them,
make them have baths. I hope all the
dolphins will stay alive for a long time. We
should ask the Earth if it's okay to put our
houses where we want them to go, because it
might be a place where we hurt the Earth or a
plant. Take care of the Earth.
Anya Rauchle, 6

I think we kids should have a little more freedom and we should be listened to a little more and be respected and be treated more equally. Maybe parents should have a little more rights, but it shouldn't be like *they* are **kings and queens** and *we* are just their servants.
Karl Bach, 11

...ask my soldiers to make a bunch of new houses for the homeless.

Michelle Leason, 10

...convince people to not drink in the streets. I'd have people build homes for other people.
Thomas Medicinehorse, 12

If I were the King or Queen of th...

...make it be so there would be no cars; instead, there would be electric fields that would pull you along. Everyone would ride bikes and you'd go down the hill but there'd be some electric field that would pull you up again. So you wouldn't have to ride up the hill. You'd just ride everywhere and there'd be electric planes and solar stuff. I think we should find a really good president. A good president wouldn't want to go to war.
Luke Garrison, 13

...help everyone in the world because the world is our home.

Anya Rauchle, 6

...make sure everyone had electric cars so we wouldn't have to care about gas, and we wouldn't have as many wars as we do now, and we wouldn't hurt our environment. I'd make sure we couldn't cut down trees or hurt or kill animals. No one would be allowed to go poaching or hunting. You shouldn't cut down trees because they take the carbon dioxide out of the world and give back fresh oxygen. I would also make sure people used solar energy.
Lauren Steinbaum, 12

...not spend a lot of money on weaponry but spend it on people. Help people who need help. Your life is not as long as you think, so you should do as much good as possible.
Josh Herman, 10

...make the world safe. I would try to stop wars all over the world and I would disarm all chemical and nuclear weapons. Most people fight about something they want or that they think is theirs or for something that was taken from them: basically, just try not to take something by force.
Alon Sacks, 9

...find cures for diseases like cancer and other life-threatening diseases. I'd stop wars. I'd try to solve problems. War is usually bad, and it's for no reason. People just get hurt for no reason.
Danny Sacks, 11

...ask for everyone to be caring of others, to the environment, to animals and plants. Caring is acting with compassion towards other beings. For example, say someone is about to be run over by a bus—instead of letting them get run over you would pull or push them out of the way. That's compassion.
Miles Ceralde, 12

...give people money and food.
Tifton Medicinehorse, 11

world with unlimited powers, I would...

...cure all diseases, like AIDS and cancer. I'd also colonize other planets so that we could house people somewhere when it got too crowded here. I'd like us to have a happier world. Live happy.
Adrian Franco, 11

...like the world to be more peaceful and have life be nice. We should plant more flowers and trees and make more parks around the world.
Evan Cranston, 9

...make gun control. I really strongly don't believe in guns and bombs and weapons of any kind.
Sarah Wiener, 13

If I were the King or Queen of the

...have cars be electric and not run on gas. I would take all the people that smoke and chew tobacco out of the world because they set a bad reputation for kids, and then when the kids grow up they might want to smoke or chew tobacco and they might kill themselves by doing that. And then those kids would set the reputation for the younger kids and it would just keep going.
Robert Lehmann, 9

...stop killing wild endangered animals and investing in tobacco. I think we should start investing more in education and schools and the homeless, instead of tobacco and crap we don't even need.
TJ Dempsey, 11

...donate some of my stuff to the poor and unfortunate kids that they would enjoy and like to play with. I feel very bad for them.
Kaylie Kathleen Williams, 10

...bring world peace. You should care about the beauty of the world by cleaning it.
Kylee Larsen, 12

...tell everyone that you'd have to be nice at
least for a day, so that they could see how to
get along. Be kind.
Elena Scott, 12

...teach people to be thankful for what they
have. I treat people I love nicely and I don't
disrespect them. I treat them with care;
I'm not mean. Earth is like a person, if you
don't treat it with respect it won't be
your friend and it will get worse.
Sophie Gilchrist, 11

...shoot people with a tranquilizer gun that
would turn them into nice people. If you were
nice to people, they would probably be nice
to you.
Mattias Hanson, 10

...make
everything be
free. No wars. Don't
be so mean. I like
animals a lot. Treat them
kindly, don't kill them. Don't bother
nature. Don't disturb animals while they're
eating or playing.
Afton Wight, 8

...end the world's hunger. I would have
supermarkets where the stuff that maybe
is really expensive in other stores could be
really cheap for people who don't have
as much money so they could still afford a lot
more food.
Lauren Christianson, 10

...take the leaders from all the countries
who want peace and have them be the king
and queen together, a united front, and
have them make all decisions together. They
would be peaceful and loving.
Siena Hood, 12

...make more houses and more stores and
get more jobs for people. I would have more
people make money, so they wouldn't
be broke, and I'd have the people sleeping
outside by themselves have a home.
Tell people to not make a mess in our world.
Gayle Henry, 12

world with unlimited powers, I would...

...make the world be pretty instead of ugly and everybody happy, and when they were sad I would have them come and discuss it.
Zoe Goldberg, 6

...make community centers for people who are sad so they could become more involved in life. Make more schools for kids.
Chelsea Cymrot, 12

If I were the King or Queen of the

...let God choose what I should do. I think that God would want us to make love and make peace and let everyone be free. Once I was alone and scared, and I prayed to God and God told me I'm never alone and everyone is always with me. If you are alone, you should pray and God will give you more love. I had a dream where God was hurt from sadness, because on Earth there were lots of people who were sad. There were angels there, I couldn't see them, they were just all this light. The angels came to help God with the sadness, and when the sadness in God was healed, then all the people of the Earth were healed too.
Amanda Slaughter, 10

...use lots of public transportation. Stop logging and re-use paper. Give money to the Third World countries.
Angelique Traub, 12

…get rid of all our missiles, and get the factories so they don't let out so much pollution, and make the logging companies leave some of the trees for the animals. I'd let all of the people who live in countries with dictators live how they want, like if they wanted to be freer. Go help people in school so they can pass.
Jeremiah Byers, 12

…raise pay for soldiers because they do so much for us. I want people to not wear furs, to save the animals. I'd want every parent who smokes to stop. It is a bad influence. Sometimes adults are too small. I think that parents should set a positive example for children.
Julia Egger, 13

…clean houses for people who are disabled, and help them get everything organized. I'd help them to get outdoors, out into the world. I'd also help people make better choices on how to live. God gave us something really special, he gave us the ability to make our own choices.
Justin Jones, 11

…shut off all power plants and have everyone use solar energy. If we don't start doing that now, global warming is going to heat up the planet and make everything die. If we keep destroying things, the Earth will fall apart. I don't want to wake up one morning and find everything in the U.S. is dead.
Lilah Clevey, 11

…be a respectful queen. I would respect everyone else and respect the Earth that we live on now. If there was a war going on I would not respect that because there are so many tragedies going on. I would probably change that and make a difference. I would make better laws like you would have to recycle and make the Earth a better place so it doesn't get trash all over it and die. We should buy trees to put in parks and pay people to clean up parks so they don't get so dirty.
Kaylie Kathleen Williams, 10

world with unlimited powers, I would…

...say no wars, no machinery that kills, no licenses for killing. Everybody would be happy. I'd pass a law for a huge fine for littering. I hope kids are having a good life and if they're not I'd be deeply depressed and I would help to raise money for them for a better life.
Spencer Palmer, 10

...make peace in the world. I wouldn't let people fight. I would make them sit down and settle it out. I would give water from the clouds. It would make rainwater to help the trees to live because if they die then there's no oxygen. I might give this book to my best friend Sam and his mother, Betsy, because I've known them for six years of my life, and I'm 7 years old.
Quincy Engelbrecht, 7

If I were the King or Queen of the

...make the world safe for everybody, and animals. I'd take away guns and say there should be no wars. To make the world a better place I'd say we shouldn't throw junk on the ground; and we shouldn't kill people.
Matthew Schabel, 7

...take all weapons away and I would put everybody in homes, not let anybody be homeless, and make all the bad guys lighten up and do something to not be bad anymore. If we don't have weapons, there's no way they can be bad. There aren't really bad children. They don't kill anyone; it's usually grown-ups. I would recommend that you not kill anybody. I would recommend that we not make bad movies, like killing movies. I would have something to prevent people from drinking heavily and driving. I'd take all cigarettes away. I would help the animals that are on the street, and if they have any wounds I'd take them to the veterinarian.
Danielle Schatzman, 8

...first try to have everybody find their inner peace and
kindness and inner strength, that they might not know about,
and show those things so that they could help people
around them. I just hope that one day everybody in the world
will be happy and peaceful and loving. We can all start with
ourselves: be as kind and caring as you can be. We should take
more care of our planet. If we use all of our resources and
aren't very careful then there won't be a good planet for the
future generations. Everybody should take an initiative to keep
the planet clean. It would be important to make sure that
everybody in the world knows how their food is grown, to be
aware of the pesticides on our food, and to grow our own food,
like in community gardens.
Elsinore Smidth, 13

...bring people from different countries to another country
so they could see how people live and maybe that can spread
around the world. That might help peace, because people
can get a sense of how other people live, in other cultures. Kids
in school are taught to not fight, to talk it over. Grown-ups are
so far from school they don't really do that anymore. That leads
to more wars and fights. It would be a better world if there was
a lot more peace.
Alexandra Goldstein, 10

world with unlimited powers, I would...

...be sure that everyone had enough to eat and a
place to sleep and that every child had parents that took care of them and that
we all had friends and shared things so that no one would steal or hurt anyone
else. We would all share what we had and all enjoy everything. I also wish that
all kids had parents like me who love them and love to be with them all the time.
Lauren Moscarello, 8

Even if it's not good now, there is always the hope to get a better life. There's other people in the world who believe for you, who want to help. Have hope and love everyone you know. Believe that it will turn out okay, even if it's not good now. If you don't like someone, try to respect their position. Maybe you'll learn that you really like them. That's how the whole world unites.
Elena Scott, 12

I don't like it when people take money away from all the schools so we can't buy supplies and paper. People shouldn't cut down trees because then the animals on the trees die.
Aaron Stone, 8

You can go to an old folks home and sing, that's what I like to do. I used to do that for my grandpa and it made everybody there feel really good. That helps. Everybody would gather around and my Uncle Bobby would play piano and sing and it really cheered them up and that felt good. It goes back to love. If you love somebody, they'll love you back.
Carrie Brandon, 9

I'd have people read more books and drink more tea. It's important to slow down and relax. In today's society, people are very uptight and rush around. To have time to sit and read and drink tea is a calming way to just sink into life. Laughter is the best thing. I laugh a lot, a really really lot. People should laugh more. Don't take things so seriously. And question authority: it helps you to be strong and to have a barrier to protect yourself; and it helps you to know what's going on.
Zoe Loughran Brezsny, 12

Use only as much money as you need. Millionaires have a lot of money, they should only use stuff that they need instead of buying humongous mansions and stuff like that.

Tyler Briant Nierstedt, 6

Don't be too hard on children when they get into trouble.

Jill Meserve, 11

You can't always take; you have to give.

Sophia Gilchrist, 11

Never give up. If you give up, you never realize your goals in life.

If the world could be one way,

I would choose the nicest way.

If the world could be one way,

I would choose the happiest way.

If the world could be one way,

I would choose the funniest way.

If the world could be one way,

I would choose the peaceful way.

If the world could be one way,

I would choose the loving way.

If the world could be one way.

Lauren Moscarello, 8

Recognize the spirit of **love** and oneness with
the universe that exist within you.
Do not make war. Be peaceful.
Do not harm others.
Don't trash Mother Earth by littering or polluting her air and water.
Keep the environment clean.
Treat animals well and don't destroy their habitats.
Preserve forests.
Distribute wealth. Care for children.
Help the homeless. **Feed the poor.**
Provide education, housing, and healthcare for everyone.
Do community service.
Laugh a lot.
Be kind and caring.
Respect all life.

Stewart Gruen **Taylor Childers** Terry Castleman

Matthew Schabel Mattias Hanson

Bragg Marcus Christianson Marshall Levensohn Sarah Wiener **Schuyler Yedlin** Siena Hood **Sophia Scorcia**

Zane Schobinger Zoe Goldberg Zoe Loughran Brezsny

Roza Trilesskaya **Samantha Collins** **Gabriel Newbrun-Mintz** Gayle Henry **Gigi Staubitz** Haley Pacheco **Indigo George**

Wagner Eric Brandon **Evan Cranston** Evan Steinbaum Albert Brown Alex Leason Alex Rauchle Alexander Palmer

Anji Herman **Anya Rauchle** Ari Bental Ariel Filane

Aaron Stone Abbie Benford Adrian Franco Afton Wight Amy Elizabeth Royal Angelique Traub

Lauren Moscarello Lauren Steinbaum Leah Grillo Liesel Staubitz

Goldstein Alon Sacks Amanda Slaughter Amy Elizabeth Royal Lauren Christianson **Lauren Grieve**

Juan Bernardo Uscategui Quincy Engelbrecht

Nicole Childers

Victoria Berggren Lucia Simon Nadia Herman

Sophia Simon **Sophie Gilchrist**

na Lynch Emma Rubinowitz **Lucinda Watson** Lucy Black **Molly McCann** Jill Meserve **Josh Herman** Joshua Slaughter

Spencer Palmer

Lucy Black Luke Garrison Luke Bennett Kaylie Kathleen Williams **Kylee Koenig** Kylee Larsen

Ciro Podany Tiffon Medicinehorse

Elena Crowe Elena Scott Eli Newbrun-Mintz

Carrie Brandon Chelsea Cymrot Danielle Schatzman

Lila Hood Lilah Clevey Lilly Barnett Miles Ceralde Moki Kawaguchi Jeremiah Byers Jacqueline Norton **Katherine Mary Scotnicki** Elena Crowe Elena Scott **Thomas Medicinehorse**

Theo Chamberlain Cali Slepin Connor Barnett Cortnay Cymrot Danielle Schatzman

ax Goodley Michelle Leason Jacob Dortman Danny Sacks Eden Knodel Eleanor Silverstein Elena Bakar Eli Newbrun-Mintz **Caleb Mahoney** Benny Bakar Danny Sacks Eden Knodel Eleanor Silverstein Elena

Elena Bakar

Isabel Rauchie Rachel Knodel Robert Lehmann **Tyla Doolin** Tyler Briant Nierstedt **Elliott Stone** Elsinore Smidth

Cole Page

nay Cymrot **Danielle Schatzman** Julia Egger **Justin Jones** Karl Baeth Tyler Briant Nierstedt **Tyla Doolin** **Tyler Mahoney** Ben Herrick Audrey Norton Eden Knodel Eleanor Silverstein Elena

Cole McCann-Phillips

Claire Lipsman

Timothy Josh Royal TJ Dempsey

Epilogue

DEBORAH MASTERS

Children are life's most precious gift to the world. They embody the universal spirit of life, and thus life's wisdom. I am proud and honored to bring the heart and soul of these 123 kids to the world. Their voices speak for the wisdom of kids everywhere. As you wander through the pages of this beautiful book, may you experience what I did as I helped create it—may you laugh and cry, swim in awe and wonder, and fill to overflowing with joy and love. I hope their words will inspire you to look deeply into your own heart, and to then act with wisdom and love towards all who live on this Earth.

ROBERT RABBIN

When I was 12 years old and living in Italy, I wrote an essay for school entitled, "What I Would Do If I Had Lots of Money." Among other things, I said I would try to make people happy. This book fulfills that aspiration, for I believe with all my heart that it will bring happiness to many millions of people. I am grateful to present the unruly and still free wisdom of these kids to the world. I pray their words will have unlimited reach and range and that all who read will heed. These kids are worthy standard-bearers for all children everywhere. Let us honor them by listening, and learning.

GLOBAL TRUTH PUBLISHING
20 Sunnyside Avenue, Suite A-116
Mill Valley, CA 94941-1928 USA
Phone 415.263.4829
Fax 415.331.2265
E-mail
sales@globaltruthpublishing.com

ADDITIONAL COPIES of this book
can be purchased through
bookstores, online bookstores, or
directly from the publisher's
website at
www.globaltruthpublishing.com.

WHOLESALE DISCOUNTS are
available to resellers and special
discounts are available on bulk
purchases of this book for
educational and fundraising
purposes and for use as
premiums, incentives, and
promotions. For details, please
contact the publisher.

A portion of the profits of this book will
be donated to organizations whose work
benefits the lives of children.